Whispers of Hope

An empowering testimony
of
transformation
Poetry.

Sally Menzies

Blackheath Dawn Publishing

Hafren House, Blackheath, Wenhaston. Suffolk IP19 9HB

Email: enquiries.blackheathdawn@gmail.com

All rights reserved. No part of this book may be reproduced or transmitted in any form without written permission of the author

Sally Menzies has asserted her moral right to be identified as the author of **Whispers of Hope**

© **Sally Menzies 2018**

ISBN   978 1911368359

This is a work of creative poetry and is intended to entertain, maybe disturb, but definitely to help and inform. In no way is it intended to defame any person, living, dead, or fictional.

For more information on the author:

www.whispersofhopepoetry.com

Scripture quotations marked NIV are taken from The Holy Bible, New International Version® NIV®

Copyright © 1973, 1978, 1984, 2011 by Biblica, Inc. ™

Used by permission. All rights reserved worldwide.

Scripture quotations marked NKJV are taken from the New King James Version.

Copyright © 1982 by Thomas Nelson, Inc.

Used by permission. All rights reserved.

Preface

In 2014, God gave me a specific Word regarding the call He has placed on my life.
It is Isaiah 61:1 – 3 (NKJV):

> *"The Spirit of the Lord God is upon Me,*
> *Because the Lord has anointed Me*
> *To preach good tidings to the poor;*
> *He has sent Me to heal the brokenhearted,*
> *To proclaim liberty to the captives,*
> *And the opening of the prison to those who are bound;*
> *² To proclaim the acceptable year of the Lord,*
> *And the day of vengeance of our God;*
> *To comfort all who mourn,*
> *³ To console those who mourn in Zion,*
> *To give them beauty for ashes,*
> *The oil of joy for mourning,*
> *The garment of praise for the spirit of heaviness;*
> *That they may be called trees of righteousness,*
> *The planting of the Lord, that He may be glorified."*

I believe that every person is unique, coming from different backgrounds and having diverse experiences in life, which shape who they are as a person. Factors from my own life persuade me to undertake a path in life where I can assist, empower, encourage and support people to find the freedom to be themselves. It has always been my desire to see and assist people to set goals, reach for their dreams and enjoy the best life possible for them. I aspire to bring people hope, to be someone who understands when it seems like no one else does, to believe in people thus helping them to believe in themselves, and to reach people wherever they are in life. One of the ways in which I can fulfil my calling in life is to use the gifts God has given me to reach others.

Writing is my primary passion and part of my calling in life. Since 1998 when I first began writing, I have considered my ability to write a blessing, and have wanted to share it with others. It has always been my dream to have my poetry published. But more importantly, it is my dream to encourage and bring hope to others through my written words.

Sally Menzies

Foreword

Not so much a collection of poetry as a deeply personal and revealing prayer diary expressed in poetic form. Sally's journey scales the heights and depths of personal realisation and expresses both joy and disappointment in accessible language that many will understand and empathise with. As part of the healing process, this work has been an essential part of Sally's re-emergence from some very dark moments. Throughout, her deep love of – and encounter with – God, is a touchstone. Sally's acceptance of the unconditional grace of Jesus continues to be a catalyst of profound transformation toward peace and wholeness.

The poetic imagination can be a lifeboat in an open and frightening sea. Sally's understanding that she was never alone may well inspire others who find themselves rocked by life's waves.

Vanessa Daughtry
Clin. couns. MA. couns. prac. BA vis. arts. PACFA.

Acknowledgements

First, I would like to thank God for blessing me with this gift that I may help bring hope and encouragement to others. It is only with His strength, grace and love, which have made all things possible for me to write this book.

I would like to express thanks to my family, for their love and support through the journey and for being an inspiration in my life.

A special thanks to Terry Gilbert-Fellows and Blackheath Dawn Publishing for making the publication of this book possible.

Recognitions to Cassandra Hollis (Storm Design) for the cover illustration and for assisting in the placement of images throughout the book to add the final touches.

My beloved, Karen Barnes, my best friend and greatest encourager. I only believe in destiny because of you. Thank you for pursuing my dreams with me and persevering, always - *Come What May.*

Sincere thanks to my cousin Sarah Pomeroy. You continued to believe in me and support me through the enjoyable and challenging times. Your acceptance and encouragement help me to be the person I am today, and have inspired me to write for and encourage others who may need the same support.

To those who have contributed to the journey but are no longer a part of it; those who were a part of the journey for a moment, a reason, or a season but whom are no longer beside me. You are a significant part of this journey because in your absence I discovered my own strength, and I learned the true love and dependability of my God. It has been in the darkest and most alone moments that I have experienced the most meaningful healing and growth, and gained some of the greatest inspiration to write these verses.

And to everyone else who has been a part of the journey so far, thank you too! You are special and unique. I appreciate all moments of creativity, revelation and reassurance; no matter how small.

Contents

Preface III
Foreword V
Acknowledgements VI
Contents VIII
If Faith Can Move The Mountains 1
   Christianity 3
   I Believe 4
   Unwanted 5
   Jesus Christ 6
   Ready 7
Life: Discovering Its Purpose 9
   I Have Learnt 10
   Journey 12
   This Life 14
   Solution? 15
   Life 17
   Life is Precious 19
   Hungry for You 21
Overcoming Depression 25
   Want To Know 26
   Trapped 27
   Imprisoned 27
   Storm 28
   What? 29
   Death 30
   Heaven 30
   Dying Inside 31
   Never Again 32
   Anymore 33
   A Hopeless Pattern 34
   The End 35
   They Don't Know 36
   Wish 37
   Relief 38

  Complete in You 39
Challenging Relationships **41**
  Bad Influence 42
  Desiderate 43
  Him 45
  His Way 46
  Crossed the Line 47
  What Changed 49
  Another Love 50
  You 51
  I Forgive You 52
The Road To Self-Discovery **55**
  Fear 56
  Afraid 57
  All I Need 60
  Stuck 61
  Voices 62
  Feel 64
  Independent 65
  Woman 66
  Choices 67
  Identity 69
  Façade 71
Don't Give Up **73**
  Success 74
  Dreams 75
  Forgiveness 75
  Hidden Talents 76
  Hardships 76
  Courage 77
  Hope 79
  Tears 79
The Faithfulness Of God **81**
  Only You 82
  Who? 83
  Home Sweet Home 83
  Whenever I Need Someone 84
  God is with Me 85
  Set Free 86
  Learning to Trust 87
  Praise God 89
  Never Let Me Go 91

Rescued	93
Young Lives for You	95
No Words	97

New Perspectives ... 99

Sometimes	100
This World	101
A New Perspective	103
Faith	105
Do We Care?	107
Is Seeing Believing?	109
Abnormality	110

Matters of The Heart ... 113

Love is Like a Disease	114
Empty-Hearted	115
Lonely Heart	116
Agonising Pain	117
Heartache	118
See You Later	119
Needs	120
Inspiration	121
Always	122
Saviour	123

A Friend For Life ... 125

True Friendship	126
Both Ways	127
Call on Me	127
You and Me	128
Together Forever	128
Another Sister	129
Dearest Friend	130
Eternity	131
Friends	132
If I were an Angel	133

Love: A Partner For Life ... 135

Memory of the Rose	136
Infatuation	138
Heart's Desire	140
Made Whole	141
Two Hearts	141
Be with Me	142
The Best Thing	143
Love	144

Encountering The Spirit **147**
   Within Reach 148
   Tears for You 150
   Intimate Spirit 150
   In the Moment 151
   Hidden 152
Walk By Faith **155**
   Live and Let Live 156
   Follow God 157
   Do Not Sin 158
   Falling Apart 159
   I Choose 161
   In The Wilderness 162
   We Will Rise 164
   Through The Day 165
Alphabetical Index **167**

If Faith Can Move The Mountains

Jesus said to him, "If you can believe, all things are possible to him who believes".

MARK 9:23 (NKJV).

Christianity

When I think of Christianity
I think of loving not hating
I think of giving not taking
I think of praying and practicing
I think of worship and praise
I see a new way of living
I see new opportunities
Morals, not restrictions
I think of grace and forgiveness
I think of repentance and truth
I feel renewed and born-again
I feel fulfilled not empty
But, most of all I think of Jesus
And I thank God
For His most perfect and precious gift.

I Believe

Jesus, you died for us
And I believe
God, you made life
And I believe
Lord, you love all things
Great and small
And of course, I believe.

Father, you watch over us
And you know when we do wrong
I need to be sorry Father,
I truly do
Love to you Lord,
Forever, Amen.

Unwanted

Satan be gone
Your place is not here
We need not evil
For God is with us
And will never leave.

Satan be gone
For the Holy Spirit lies within
We need not hate, but love
And through Jesus we receive.

Satan be gone
For our faith is in God
As He gives us hope
And we are purely forgiven.

Satan be gone
For God gave us
His only begotten son
And whoever believes in Him
Shall not perish
But have eternal life.

Satan be gone
Your time is never
Jesus is coming
And we are saved.

Jesus Christ

To make it through this day
I say a little prayer
As I place my life in God's hands
Knowing He will protect me
It is written in His word
Holding strongly to faith
Nothing can tear it away from me
Not Satan or his hosts or anything else
For, I believe in Jesus Christ
He makes all things possible
I have been forgiven for my sins
While it should have been me
It was Jesus Christ upon that cross
God's ultimate sacrifice,
my price has been paid
I should have been dead and buried
But my Lord my God has let me live
Through all I have experienced
Nothing has felt more real than the truth
Truth, Jesus himself allowed me to see
Is why I am living now
I will proclaim my testimony of God
With every chance I get
Because I believe in Jesus Christ
If I wake to see tomorrow
I will say a little prayer of thanks
Because each day is truly a blessing
And life's purpose is yet to be fulfilled.

Ready

Thanks to God for my second chance,
For letting me live, enjoy my life,
Yearning to see it fulfilled.
When Jesus returns, I will be ready.
Life is so precious
I never want it to end
Afraid it may end sooner than I hope
Willing to go when Jesus calls me
Accepting Christ's invitation
Living to His will:
For Christ and Christ alone
Praying each day,
He will Let me live one more day
Every day thanking Him for the chance
To freely live another day.
I give my life to Jesus
For whom I live
Through good and bad
Trusting in Jesus
Whatever life brings
Standing by Jesus
I will be ready
When Jesus returns.

Life: Discovering Its Purpose

For each negative there is a positive.
Life is sometimes hard but there is always hope.

I Have Learnt

Love so strong
I have been searching for
Now have found my way.

I have learnt to be myself
No matter what the cost
Because I cannot be anyone else
I have learnt that faith keeps us hoping
And hope keeps us living.

I have learnt that the choices
I face Are only for me,
even if they do affect others
I have learnt that seeing is only believing
Because believing is seeing.

I have learnt that we do not know what is right
Until we have experienced what is wrong
I have learnt that wishing
doesn't change anything
It is when we reach for our dreams
that we achieve.

I have learnt that we can rejoice in
the saddest times
Because the ultimate price has already
been paid
I have learnt that we can fall on our own
But we cannot stand on our own.

I have learnt that we get many chances in life
But when we die no more chances
And above all, I have learnt that
you cannot love anyone
Until you love your creator and yourself.

Journey

Life is not a game
It is a journey
Take it seriously
Don't mess with it
You can become lost
So trust the right one to guide you.
If you are lost
Find the correct track
Because if you have faith
You can always find a way

There is no return
Go forward
Not always certain
Of the destination,
You have hope
For what it will be
For hope lasts forever
Whilst disappointment fades.

You have expectations
Which are not always met
But you keep moving on.
So much to see
So much to do
Make the most of it
Enjoy it
There will be pitfalls
Occasional bad weather
Sure knowledge of clear sky
And sunshine yet to come.
For every journey,
There is an end,
Be prepared
For what awaits you
When your journey of life
Is complete.

This Life

Time to die
Pass this life over
A new one to begin
A separate life of my own
I can only dream of
Given up on all hope
Want to turn this life around
No hope left within
Time to give it all up
Throw this life of mine away
And give them reason to complain
They will not chastise me anymore
This life of mine will be gone
No more need to worry
I am going to end it all
The end of all my pain,
The end of all my
burdens.

Solution?

Where is that person I used to be?
Why have I changed for the worse?
I no longer care about anything
I no longer know who I am
I no longer know where I am heading
I no longer know what I want.
Used to be full of inspiration
Full of love
Now, full of heartache and pain
Seeing no solution but death.
If I die, I leave this lonely world
It would make my friends so sad
But many others would be glad.

Leaving this world,
My present problems would
melt so quickly away
But, then I would face eternal death
And not get a chance
For what God has to offer.
Death seems like my only solution
But it is not a solution at all
I guess I must live this life
Of fear, loneliness,
All the hurt, all the pain
Until I truly go insane
Presently on the verge
Of falling apart
My friend, please
Hold me close, keep me sane
And never leave
Until my time is through.

Life

Life Precious;
Has such meaning
Life, beautiful
A gift from God
Better when lived for Him
Life, a journey
Of trial and suffering
Happiness and joy
Tears and laughter
Life is what we make of it
And what we have
Going to end
Only lived once
Life, full of surprises
is not worth giving away
But worth everything you have.

Life, although not easy
Is survivable
Not a game;
Serious
Also fun
Emotional
Spiritual
Physical
Mental
Life can be complicated
And cherished
Life, so wonderful
Often taken for granted
Always changing
Full of hopes and dreams
Life, enjoyable
Full of different experiences
Is an invitation to live God's way.

Life is Precious

I know you are hurting so much right now
But there is a rainbow still to come
We are both missing a lot of each other
But our friendship will always remain strong
I wish I could be the one
Who is with you every day,
To wipe away your tears,
To hold you when you are weak
And catch you when you fall
I cannot take away your burdens
But I can help you carry them
Do not throw away what you have
It is not worth losing
Do not throw away your life
You may not realise it now
But life is precious
And there is so much more
That you have to offer.

I can be your friend forever
If you just let me
We can grow old together
If you just give life a chance
I promise you will remain in my heart
Whichever way you choose
I will be thinking of you forever
Whether you are physically with me or not
You can always find a way
To make this life of yours more successful
But you have to take a chance
If you take the chance to live your life
You will eventually understand
That your life was meant to be
The more we grow together
The more we can understand each other
But currently, this option lies in your hands.

Hungry for You

I am hungry for your presence
Hungry for your touch
hungry for your love Lord,
I am hungry for you.

I want to know the one who gave it all
Died to save us from sin
Because in Him, my heart beats again
Now I live to bring praise
hungry to know you God.

Nothing else can satisfy
Nothing can compare
Nothing could I want more
you are all I ever need.

You alone are the one I seek
You alone are my desire
I seek to know your heart
to do as you please
Longing to see your face Lord
Hungry to know you more.

Lord, you loved me first
called me by name
Created in your image
I have been chosen by you
When I cry, you wipe my tears
In my joy, you dance with me.

You showed me how to live
How precious you are to me
Ever loving, faithful
Glorious is your name
Divine and true
I hunger for more of you.

Overcoming Depression

*"I have told you these things, so that in me you may have peace.
In this world you will have trouble.
But take heart! I have overcome the world."*

JOHN 16:33 (NIV).

Want To Know

I want to know
How love feels
Feel it myself.
I want to know
How success feels
What fun is
Have some.

I know too well
How hate feels
How failing feels
Now I want to succeed.
Never known fun
Always known pride.

I want to know
What right is
How good feels
Fed up with the bad
All of this I've never known
Now I want to know.

Trapped

Why do things
Always happen this way?
Always aimed at me.
I cannot escape the blame
For it has me trapped
Trapped in the corner of insanity.
I cannot get a grip on life
There is nothing left for me.
Is this life I'm living
Really worth the pain
Or is it worth giving it away
With anything I've got?

Imprisoned

The truth is always hidden
Too difficult to find
With no hope left within
Faith is running slim
Imprisoned by troubles and fears
The light has faded out
Insanity drawing nearer
Shall never be free.

Storm

Hear thunder
See rain
See lightning
Flash the sky.

Everything seen
Blurry
Nothing clear
Near or far.

Stuck in this storm,
Nowhere to go,
Which way is home?
Which way is safe?

Darkness arising
Out of the sky
Creeping into world
Snuffing out light.

Heart struck by lightning
Thunder rumbles, deafening
Soul soaked by rain
The storm, is life.

What?

What is going on?
I cannot think!
Sounds of fear
Running through my mind.

I have no vision
On what is near
I can't even see
Any distant light.

Where am I?
And what am I doing?
knowing that somehow
this terror must be stopped

With thoughts and visions
Crossing my mind
I cannot understand
What any of them mean.

Nothing lasts forever
Eyes opened, I am free!
From all the hurt and pain
That once caused me to hate.

Death

Light, the enemy
Darkness, friend.
Cold arms
Wrapped around neck.
Grip hard
Strong
Life is gone forever
Freedom, a mystery.

Heaven

Heaven
A better place
The end of all crisis
The end of all tears
No worry or misunderstanding
No sorrow or guilt
A place of love righteousness

Here in the hearts of loved ones
Forever in their thoughts

Yet, physically out of this world
Permanently absent from evil and sin.

Dying Inside

Dying inside
No screams to be heard
What can be done to help?
When no-one is there
Except, loneliness and emptiness...

Who cares?
No-one understands
Those who try to help
Only help themselves.
No hope for some.

When dying inside
Nothing seems to matter
Nothing ever makes a difference...
Existing, not being
Lost mind, body and soul.

Never Again

Never Again
Wanting to face another day
While still trying
To understand life.

Never again
Hoping to look forward
To enjoyable events
To see things crash down again

Never again
Daring to love
Another heart and soul
Better forgotten.

Never again
Will to live
When life is over
Thanks to God
First, last
Only one life.

Anymore

All the hurt and despair
Waves crushing in
Too much to handle
Cannot take anymore.
Need a grasp on life
A load of fresh air
Need to stop the trembling;
Shaking all throughout
Prevent the tears from falling
Fear from seeping out
Pain has taken over
Cannot take anymore.
End this terror
Still keep life
Desperately praying
Cannot take anymore.

A Hopeless Pattern

Life has a hopeless pattern
Hard to manage alone
Holding on to faith and hope
Yet a stranger to this life.
An unfolding pattern
Birthing negativity
Intoxicated with darkness
Horrid depths, lows of life
Like a person living
In a world of insanity
Something wrong, seriously wrong
That which is missing
Cannot be found
When what is missing,
Is unknown,
Life's hopeless pattern
Drives me senseless
Living life correctly
Isn't meant to be.

The End

Life dragging on
Every day, more bad than good
letting go of hope
not trusting anymore
refusal to love again

Dreams crushed
closed heart
From expressing emotion
mind shut off
From positive thoughts.

Inside dead, buried
still wandering around
fear never ending
life ending too soon.

They Don't Know

They don't know what I am going through
Don't know how I feel,
Don't see it through my eyes
Nor are they the ones being treated like this
They don't hear what my ears hear
Don't feel the pain my heart feels
Don't know what it is like
And don't want to understand.

They can block it out of their knowledge
Cannot read my thoughts
They don't know what is happening to me
And don't want to care
They only see what they want to see
Only choose to believe the lies
They won't even accept the truth.

It is me who is rupturing with pain
Suffering the lies
Bearing these heavy loads
I see through my eyes and know what I think.
No-one but me knows my hearts agony.

They don't care, they don't believe
They don't see, don't feel it
It is happening to me, not to them
I am the one dying, they have lives to live
This is me, it is my death
They cannot help me live my life again.

Wish

I wish that I could run and hide
Far, far away from here
From this place of terror
A constant cauldron of fear.

I wish that I could shake away
The disappointment, the misery.
Find a solemn place
Of peace, love and happiness.

I wish I could take away the pain
Wash away the tears
Run through the wind
To blow it away.

I wish I could swim the ocean
To wash it away
Build a bridge to get over it
Climb a mountain
To reach the highest point.

Anything at all
To rid this life
Of loneliness,
Pure emptiness.

Relief

Finally cried
let it all out told
All there is to tell showed
That hidden smile
laughed
About the horrible past
finally let go
Of all the misery withheld
To cherish
The beauty of this world
Understand this life of mine.

Complete in You

Called out of darkness
Into light
Released from pain
Fears overcome through you
Brought into a new place of hope.
Covered me
With mercy, grace
Healed the brokenness
Carried through weakness
Strengthened
Joy brought to life
Remembering
How you saved me
Wrapped in your love
Blessed with
your presence

Made new by your spirit
I am complete in you.

Challenging Relationships

*"But to you who are listening I say:
Love your enemies,
do good to those who hate you,
bless those who curse
you, pray for those who mistreat you."*

LUKE 6:27 – 28 (NIV).

Bad Influence

A bad influence? Am I?
How can that be?
I never discouraged honesty
Never encouraged bad habits
I hold a special strength
Only want to share it
Yet I am being accused
Of being nothing but a bad influence
Tell me why it is me
Who is so falsely accused?
Always cast away
Until I speak out loud
What they don't want to hear
Am I a bad influence?
Does she believe it's true?
Shall I stand up with the truth?
Or let her believe the lie?

Desiderate

Having met someone
Especially drawn to
Unable to explain it
But strong feelings I have.

So much time spent
Just thinking about you
Conjuring images in my mind
Even dreaming of you.

Seeing you, smiling
Being around you makes the day better
Everything seems
Bearable, worthwhile.

Not understanding the attachment
Only wanting to be close to you
Longing to know you more
A significant someone in your life.

Wanting so much to be your friend
Trust, confide
Yearning to be there for you
As you were there for me.

Thoughts, emotions
Almost torturous
Fighting hard to hold on
Ever fearing losing you.

I can only hope
You feel the same
Having the relationship desired
You will never let me go.

Him

Tears rolled down her face
Terrified
What he had done
Just wasn't fair
He made her feel cold
Fearful inside
She didn't know
How to face him
He got very offended
By a simple grin.

But, she left him
All by himself
Could not handle it anymore
All too much
Her life now
Is turned around
Enlightened, lifted up
Totally free
Able to do what she wants
Whenever she wants.

His Way

She took him into her arms
He abused her love
He had hurt her
So deep within her heart.
She did not know
What he came for
Now realising
It was all for his pleasure.
He did not care
What she wanted.
He went ahead
Without her consent.
He knew quite well
That it was wrong
It made no difference
He liked it much better
If things went this way
Nothing she said or did
Would ever make a difference.

Crossed the Line

I always thought that people could
Have opposite sex friends
I fooled myself to believe
That people understood boundaries
That people have values
Know where the line is
And not to cross it.
I met you; I thought I found a friend
Then I discovered who you really were.

You used my kindness as weakness
Took advantage of my vulnerability
You played on my emotions and
Got inside my head.
You preyed on me
Yet I blamed myself
Asking questions of why and what if
Trying to work out where I went wrong
But no matter what I did or said
I couldn't stop how you felt
Or what you did.

You crossed the line, mistreated me
Our relationship broken, along with others
Endless days I spent trying
To get you out of my head
You placed the guilt trip on me
Still, I tried to protect you.
You'd talk to me
Saying things you shouldn't say
Made me wonder where your morals were
I told you the truth
You didn't want to hear
I re-marked the boundaries
Again, you crossed the line.

The vicious cycle made me dizzy
Round and round, no end in sight
One of us had to leave
Part of me always knew
It would be me
But don't think you have won
Don't think this is the end of me.
I had to walk away
But, you can't hold me down
I will prove, in the end
You didn't get the better of me
I am stronger and wiser
And will fight for others like me
For what you did to me was not fair
And no one should have to put up with that.

What Changed

Sometimes I wonder
Why our love couldn't work
And how I remember
How happy we were then.

The smile on your face,
The tears in your eyes,
Every single emotion
Brought love to my heart.

You were always there
When I needed someone,
Your precious kiss
Upon my sweetened lips.

Whenever we touched
A tender sensation,
Filled our souls with comfort
Overwhelmed our hearts with joy.

So, what changed the way
That you and I used to be?
We were the sweetest couple
And the very best of friends.

Another Love

To fall in love with another
You say was not fair
And I know what you say is true
But I need someone who
Can be with me often
I need a relationship that God would permit
I'm sorry that it was not you I chose
It's not easy for me to see
That I have hurt you and broken your heart
But this relationship I am now in
God didn't say 'no' to
I see him whenever I please
I miss him when he's not around
I miss him when he doesn't call
I need him, he makes me happy
I'm sorry our relationship was not best for us
Can you forgive me for choosing another?
Can we maintain a friendship still strong?
Replacing a love for one another?
I still want you in my life
Only as a friend.
I have found another love
It's not easy for me to see I have hurt you
I'm sorry have broken your heart
But I know you are strong
You will survive
Once again I am sorry
For you and me
This love was never meant to be.

You

You lied to me
You hurt me
You said you loved me
You cheated
You used me
You did it behind my back
You expected me
To forgive you
And you told me
That you still love me
But you left me
For your ex-girlfriend
So, I told you
Our friendship couldn't survive
And all we ever did together
Really doesn't matter anymore.

I Forgive You

You knew my weaknesses
And you used them against me
Every time we had a fight
But, I forgive you.
I don't know what it was we had
But I know what it was not
The friendship-love relationship I wanted
And I forgive you.
You hurt me
I hurt you
And you let me go
I forgive you
Will you forgive me?

The Road To Self-Discovery

*You cannot truly be happy with someone else,
Until you are happy with yourself.*

Fear

Wandering out of sight
Through the day, through the night
Knowing not where to go
Walking fast, walking slow
Darkness, bringing creeping fear
Causes moon to disappear
Feelings, weird, lonely lost
As a cork at sea is tossed
Across the breakers of unending blight,
Aged, sickened stale mouth fright,
Unable to escape the mess
Sink, surrender my consciousness.

Afraid

Don't want to be anymore
No, don't want to be
Not saying to be someone else
That isn't what it means.

Life, it seems so hopeless
Always ending here
Constant, endless shards of pain
No solution in sight.

Running from the fear
Afraid to let go,
Inability to face it
The greatest fear of all.

Eyes afraid to open
Eyes that will not shut
Heart afraid of loving
A love that will not stop.

Mind afraid to think
Doesn't know better
Soul afraid of darkness
Fears even rainbow's arc.

Every part, whole life
Lived through fear, confusion
Constant, always, without end
Long to live without fear.

Dreaming of a brighter tomorrow
Is reality, tomorrow never to come
Strive to take one day at a time
Search, inside for freedom.

All I Need

A
Love
A love
A little love
All I need is fairness
As I search for friendship
All I need is someone to hold
A someone to hold and to help me
All I need is to experience the reality
And search within   for that real me.
Always hope I'll   always search
Always true,   so strong self
Another's strong self
Another's love

Heartfelt.

Stuck

I am stuck in this place,
Knowing nothing of where I am
My disturbed thoughts to face
Where can I turn, seek my help
Lost, lonely, no warm embrace
Yearn for understanding
I endure; yet have no understanding
Pain I feel, brought on by self,
Face a world of disruption and fears
Unease, terrors, endless to be endured,
A drowning cold implosion of tears.
Darkest memories lurch from my mind,
In this madness, stuck in this place,
Where is the help, where the escape
Losing my grip on all belief,
Is all replaced with loneliness new shape?
Am I a proof to suffering's non relief?

Voices

Head filled with multiple voices
Each fights to be heard
Growing stronger, more dominant
Unable to silence them
Results in loss of control.

On the verge of breaking point
Faith and confidence start to sway
Self becoming unrecognisable
Something inside begins to stir
Fear of the voices intensifies.

From deep within,
Something foreign, yet
Strangely familiar emerges
Guaranteed not who is presenting
Or who is in control.

Greatest ally and enemy the same
Conjured thoughts of violence
Leading to unthinkable action
Time is spent trying to silence
Be rid of the voices.

Missing links from the past
Enticed by fiendish desire
Temptation too strong to withstand
Satisfied the appetite
This is what they are capable of.

Advice sought but never taken
Strength and control never gained
If listening to the inner child
Standing ground, being assertive
Things would be different now.

Still, never too late to make a change
The past can be dealt with
Not just left behind
To reconcile those transverse traits
For the sum of all parts, is whole.

Feel

Was selfish
Stubborn
Crushed.

Guilty
Reckless
Regretful.

Now revived
Forgiven
Saved.

Loved,
Inspired
Good.

Only the
Truth feels
This real.

Independent

Independent,
My own self
No longer misjudged,
Mistreated, wrongly accused
Run free
Who I want to be
Reach dreams Succeed
Independence time arrives
Over past
Left all behind
Future to come
Present privilege
Live life
Way I want
Be independent
My own self.

Woman

A woman
Of nothing
But strength and courage
A woman
of faith
And righteousness
Learning and growing
Like a child
Living like an adult
Is what she is
Nothing, she is
not.

Choices

Look in the mirror
Recognise result of becoming
Reflect on moments that define,
Dare to change the response
Of all the hearts broken
How can they be mended?
Choosing to forgive perpetrators of pain
Without reconciling relationships
Accepting responsibility for choices, actions,
Admitting faults, humbly apologise?

Seize that inner strength
Using power to do what is right
Standing up for truth, values
Challenge demons, fight for freedom?
Take the chance to be

One of love, hope, proud to be.
In every trial, triumph
Never powerless.
With circumstances beyond control
Will to choose how to respond.
Life's challenges are shaping
Choose the example to lead.

When realisation of who I was becoming
Opposite of true, genuine,
Acknowledgment of choice followed
Continued to change for worse
Take hold of inner strength, power
Improving the self.

Become humble, accept error in ways
Realise mistakes; learn
Admit faults, apologise; forgive
Value self, life,
All your fellow travellers.

Choices made
For today, tomorrow
To be someone loved, respected
Live the best life possible today.

Identity

Let me tell you something, I
believe that there are
Too many people judging me
Telling me who they think I should be.
Some say it isn't true
Some say it's just a phase too
Maybe they should take a step
into my shoes and see
What life is like, living as me
So long filled with self-hatred and shame
To fight with oneself, they'll see is no game.
The more they tell me it isn't right
The more I want it; the more I fight
Not only to seek to prove them wrong
But to accept myself and still stand strong.
Caught in a cycle that I cannot sustain
Where to deny myself,
Yet keep my faith is my gain.

Constantly meeting others' disbelief
Revealing secrets brings no relief.
For years confusion and frustration prevailed
'Til through self-acceptance, my freedom un- veiled.
Now I boldly declare my identity
Being Christian and bisexual
brings much serenity.
Take this confession as me 'coming out'
No more contradictions, no more messing about
No more hiding, no more disguise
This is who I am.
I will not compromise.

Façade

Who is this authentic being within
That has not been discovered before?
Years wandering aimlessly
Wearing new masks to suit each situation
Masks to cover true feelings;
Masks so that no-one can see
The scared, broken person that is reality
But no matter the masks,
You see right through.
Deep within, you see
The person you created
You channel your love into hearts
Until your truth is experienced within
Eyes and ears opened
Hearts attuned to yours
Beginning to see as you do;
Beloved, accepted and free.
One by one, the masks put aside
Rest in your trust
Believing, declaring the truth
Confidence building,
Identity re-shaped
Through the eyes of love, the work of grace
I am who I am
because you said I am.
......Mask-less.

Don't Give Up

But we also glory in our sufferings, because we know that suffering produces perseverance; perseverance, character; and character, hope.

ROMANS 5:3 – 4 (NIV).

Success

Stand up for what you believe
Let no one tear you down
Reach for your goals, never give up
Once you reach one, set another
Never stop dreaming
Forever trying new things
For there is always going to be
Success and achievement ahead.
Only you can reach your dreams
No substitution can suffice
Never give up hope
There is no achievement without hope.
Never give up loving
Love wipes away much hate and sin
Always be open to new friendships
Hold strong to those already formed
Friendship, love, faith and hope
Together build the human heart.

Dreams

Although dreams are hard to follow
Never consider them out of reach
For wishes are dreams
And dreams can come true
Believe, believe, believe
Things aren't always what they seem
If dreams seem out of reach
You will reach them
If you believe.

Forgiveness

Forgiveness is the key to life
The way to move on.
Forgive; forget
Live without regret.
Forgiveness is the justification
The purity in a relationship.
When you know how to forgive
You know how it feels
To be forgiven
You will have friends for life.

Hidden Talents

You are very special
God has gifted you
You are unique
Your talents may be hidden
That does not mean
That they are non-existent
Look deep inside your heart
To find that you have
Talents beyond your imagination
Because God has gifted you
Made you special; made you unique.

Hardships

When dreams are scattered
So hard to hold on.
When hope is lost
So hard to regain.
When friendship is torn
So hard to trust.
When hearts are broken
So hard to love.
When fear takes over
So hard to have faith.
And when everything changes
It is the hardest to stay the same.

Courage

Life always has its challenges,
People trying to bring you down,
Adversity comes from all angles
Sometimes you feel all alone.

Some people's sole purpose is to test you
Others will encourage and empower you
There are ones who attempt to use you
And those that will do life with you.

Have confidence; believe in yourself
Learn to appreciate your own value
When no one else fights for you
Stand up for yourself.

Draw on your inner strength
Stand on your own two feet
You need to fight the battle
Only you can prove them wrong.

Don't let them steal your joy
Don't let them take your peace,
Find your voice
Have the courage to say no.

Don't blame yourself
Not seeing your worth is their loss,
Have the authority over your life
Make yourself a priority.

To fight your battle
Firstly, you need strength
To have strength, you must know yourself
Make time for what is good for you.

Always stand up for what you believe
Persist in reaching for your dreams
Whatever happens
Never give up on yourself.

Hope

The truth may be hidden
May be hard to find
But if you have faith
You will find what it is
Along with truth comes hope
Hope brings wonders
And wonders never cease.

Tears

Tears hurt when they fall
But they are the best gift of all
When you feel like crying
There is no need for denying
Do not hide them away
Just smile and face the next day
Tears may be hard to wrestle
But for each of us, they are special.

The Faithfulness Of God

*God has set me free
I have seen the light
And my life is in His hands
He will do the same for you
You just need to have faith.*

Only You

Only you know what is going to happen
Only you can fulfil my dreams
Only you can guide me
through the good times,
Help me through the bad times
Show me the way.

Only you know me through and through
You know all my weaknesses
And show me how to be strong.
It is you who taught me all of this
You taught me how to be strong
How to fulfil my dreams.

It is you who loved me from the start
Who showed me how to live;
Showed me how to love.
It is you on whom I can depend
Show me the light
The truth in my life.

Who?

Who is there when you need a friend?
Who is there when you need some love?
Who is there to listen to your prayer?
Who can see your every move,
Read your thoughts
And know your pain?

It is God, He is always there
When you feel in need
He knows your every move,
He is perfect,
He is your friend.

Home Sweet Home

God is always there
With open arms
Welcoming me home
In Him I place my whole trust
With Him I place my soul
He holds the key to my heart
The key to my life.

Whenever I Need Someone

Whenever I need someone
To wipe away my tears
A shoulder to lean on
With a heart to rely on
There is never one there.

Whenever I need someone
To give me a tender hug,
To turn my frown upside-down
And to make me happy again
No one ever comes.

Whenever I need someone
To care for me
And love me as a dear friend
Who is there in return
To take away my fears?
I never have anyone.

But, then I always remember
That there is someone
Who loves me all the time
And who is always there?
It is my Lord, my God
In Heaven above.

God is with Me

Once afraid
Terrified of all that life contained
Fear was controlling
Trying to dominate
But with God
Peace entered in
Not fearing anymore.

Once lost
Blinded from the truth
No right direction to go
Life, a mystery that blindness, wiped away
Now free
God is with me.

Once hopeless
Blackened with sin
Took a firm hold of me
Unable to hold any peace
The Lord, My God saved
Sins washed away
Forgiven.

Set Free

We live in a world of temptation
We live in a world of sin
But because of the blood Jesus shed
We have all been set free.
We will try not to give in to temptation
However, if we do, there is forgiveness
for our sins
Because Christ Jesus has set us free.
We are surrounded by evil
We are surrounded by hate
But evil and hate will not penetrate our souls
For God has saved us and set us free.
Within our hearts, within our souls
We are filled with comfort, love and joy
The Lord Jesus has saved us
we are set free.

Learning to Trust

Sometimes we wonder
If God can hear us,
If He really cares,
Is He even there?
If He sees our pain,
Why is He silent?
Why doesn't He interfere?

There are times
When we don't feel His presence
When church, prayer and fasting
Become mundane
We lose sight of our purpose
And the passion fades.

Still, faith remains a part of us
We know in our hearts
That He loves us,
That His promises are true
But if we cease communicating
We stop walking with Him day by day.

Yet, if we continue to praise Him
If we run to Him
Instead of running away
If we continue to pray
Listening to His word
In the darkness we will Seek
and find Him.

For even in weakness, He is our strength
His love always remains
Every morning
His mercies are new
Continually, His grace
Is sufficient for us.

So, when the cloud of doubt
Begins to cover you
Ask the Lord to show you again
How to trust Him
To teach you to stand and fight
To remind you
Who He truly is.

When we practice our faith, learn to trust
We will see, God is always there
It is times like these
Those strengthen our bond
And draw us closer to Him.

Praise God

Let the truth be revealed
To all who have ears
May they hear the word of God
Jesus Christ is coming soon
It may be today or tomorrow
It may not be for ten or twenty years or more
This tells us all to be ready
We need to stop being foolish
Open your heart to God's truth
He offers us eternity in paradise
God is the one who sent Jesus Christ
He did not send Him to condemn
He sent Him to save us
Jesus Christ died our deaths
He took our sins to the cross
So that we may be forgiven.

He brings us joy and peace
God loves us so much
That He was willing to give Jesus Christ
Do not underestimate
the power of God himself
He created us and he can destroy us
But with Christ we shall not fear
Through faith we can receive freedom
A life of love and hope
A life of opportunities not restrictions
God has set me free along with many others
And we have seen God's true glory
He will do the same for you
You just have to believe.
Praise God!

Never Let Me Go

Through God I receive forgiveness
Through Him who gave me life
No issue, no burden is too great for Him
For God held strong to me.
Through all my times of need,
Through trials, sufferings and heartaches
God never let go of me.
When my faith was running slender
My patience running out
When everything fell down
God gave me a way to make it through
He held onto me, despite my pain
He held me close, kept me from death
God never let me go.

When I felt like drowning
When I felt like giving up
God kept a firm hold on me
He never let me go.
Even when I fall to pieces
God picks me up, mends.
When I fail in my own eyes
God shows me where I succeed.
When I'm lost and lonely
God rescues me
His comfort reassures me.
To you, God, I give my praise
I worship you, I lift my hands.
You never gave up on me
You kept me holding on.
My Lord, you never let me go
I will praise you Lord,
forevermore.

Rescued

I have been told
That my faith is meaningless
My dreams will amount to nothing
There were times I started to believe them
When dreams and faith
Sat on the backbench of my life.

Somehow, I knew I still needed you
But I locked you away
In a place in my heart
Where I thought I could keep you safe
Where nothing and no one
Could take you from me.

I put you to the back of my mind
Stopped walking with you day by day
I hid you where no one could see
Then my passion faded away
I blended in with the world
Became who everyone else
Wanted me to be.

But you never forgot me
Refused to give up
You saw me through eyes of grace.
Before I knew you
I was broken, in distress
Misery, my constant companion.

When I was rescued by you
Received peace from within;
A wholeness, re-found joy of you
As sorrows melted away

And now, my God, I pledge to you
I will remember
Everything you have done for me
I was baptised in the flesh
Then you baptised me in the spirit
My sins washed away
You rescued me.

Young Lives for You

Young lives come before you
Each a story of their own
Yet their purpose is the same
They come to seek your face
To hear you speak to them.

A young one wears a mask upon their face
Carrying secrets hidden deep within
Brokenness has left scars on their hearts
They come, this day, with expectation
Of release, healing and restoration.

Trying so hard to hide out there
But here with you there is nothing to hide
Finding conviction not condemnation
Set free from their own imprisonment
Finding themselves in you.

You brought them here to you today
To reveal your love and care for them

To tell them you see their pain and understand
To teach them they are significant
And to open their hearts to you.

Here in your presence young people surrender
They receive salvation from you
With peace in their hearts,
Their joy is restored in you
Because of this newfound confidence
They now see they are accepted in your eyes.

From here they will walk
A new journey
Refreshed, alive in you
Going forth declaring your name
They live as a testament
Of your love
And find their purpose in
Bringing all glory to you.

No Words

There are no words to describe your glory
No words to describe how divine you are
Nothing I can say to explain
How precious you are to me
No way to fully express my thanks
Nothing I can do to measure
What you have given to me
What can I give to the one who gave it all?
How can I ever repay
The debt you paid for me?

Despite all the words I have
And all the actions I display
I cannot express it with my flesh
But you know me inside out
So with the fire in my heart
And the desire in my soul
I give you all of me
As the best way I know how
To express my love
And my thanks to you
For everything you have done.

New Perspectives

Do not turn around, take another perspective.
The solution is there, waiting for you to find it.
You are not looking in the right place.

Sometimes

Sometimes things get tough,
We sit, we wonder why.
If only sometimes we could change
The outlook on different situations.
If we could do this
What wonders we would be
Then, maybe,
People would see us as normal
Not so utterly strange.
If everyone changed their view
What a wonderful place this could be,
No one would be called an outcast
Everyone would be known as human
Perfectly normal in each person's eyes.
If only the world was looked after
And people were more aware;
Then this place would be
A better place for you
A better place for me.

This World

What world is this we live in?
Tearing apart, bleeding deeply
What is being done to save it?
Feel its pain
Hear the cries!

Our world, bleeding
Enduring intense pain
We need to embrace its beauty
Feel fortunate to preserve.

World, suffering
Freedom darkened with disgrace
Comfort is rare
As peace is despised
Injustice rolls in to dominate.

This world has started to shatter
people tremble with fear
What sort of world will we pass on
To the next generation, to future years?
A world of hate?
A world of cruelness, deception?

Today's decisions, for tomorrow
A world of darkness or prosperity?
Revive the world; save it?
Or let it die decay?
Not only for the world but us
To preserve or let die?
Our future is in our hands.

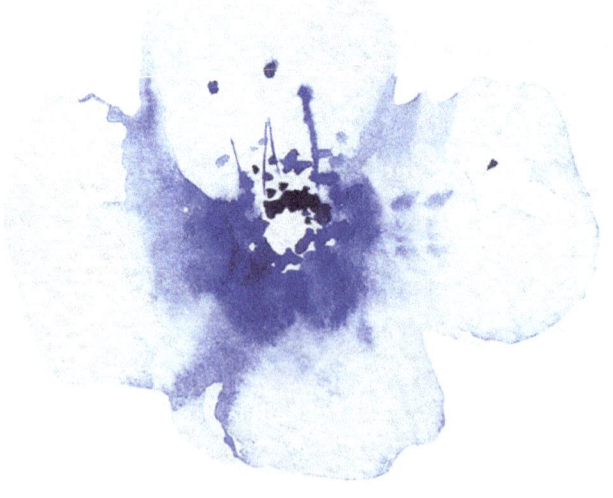

A New Perspective

Pain is excruciating
Harm has been done
Effects will last forever
Future seems dull and lifeless
The past, a horrid nightmare.

Life has lost its meaning
Death has opened opportunities
All hope is now extinguished
Faith is becoming slender

Questions preoccupy thoughts
The answers have been diminished
The inability to cope is increasing
But the solution is there waiting
It is yet to be explored.

Turn around, be haunted?
No, a new approach.
Stop, breathe, a different view
It is the perspective that is wrong.

Eyes closed
Mind opened
Sudden vertigo of emotions
Spirit freedom
Within the soul, a hidden resolution.

In the midst of emptiness, truth is revealed
Comfort found, fear released
To dream, goals achieved
Now with open eyes, the time has come
The new perspective, now, reality.

Faith

There is a love and a grace
above all else
a power so wonderful
salvation strong
There is an ultimate sacrifice a
price already been paid.

There is a secret place that is open to all
Only one can show you
Open hearts
Open minds
Will see, believe
All that is in this place is beyond imagination
Only faith can take us there.

Secrets, all revealed
All dreams captured
no need for fear
They have not been ripped away
prayers are being answered
future is being planned
Life, good - secure
past forgotten.

Forgiven, saved
living today because death was defeated
Filled with hope, love faith,
A priority
Knowing deep, sure
Truth learned
New life shared with others
Set free. To be.

Do We Care?

What, can I make of this life?
Where can I go,
what can be done to make this life
more successful?
Has everything been said, done with nothing left to try?
Outside embracing nature,
Seeing everything special and unique having
its very own way of being.
Not one tree, bird, human,
or animal,
Is exactly the same as another.

Wonder how this world came to be
realising it's not something
meant to be easily understood.
Created for each of us to enjoy not
destroy.
Changed, the world
Perfect to polluted
Crushing, killing it
Unsustainable
Does anyone care?

Nature so beautiful, still is
being ruined
Searching, protecting rubbish
environment dies.
selfish, own desires, conflicted
war, invention, destruction.
Does anyone really care?

Created in harmony,
here to help others
instead of hurting them?
Called to love not hate
But persistently going astray.

Embezzled by evil
Denying the problems lying within.
Deflecting, oppressing, exploiting
Self-assertion, compulsion, greed
Is this how the story will end?

Is Seeing Believing?

Sometimes we see things
That we can't always believe
Even after we hear
That "seeing is believing".

Do you sometimes wonder
If what you see
Is nothing but hallucination?
Can you believe it's real?

Can you close your eyes
And imagine it goes away
Only to wake up and see
That nothing was there?

Do you ever wonder
What all of this means?
Are you looking for answers
You have not yet found?
Or do you stop and think
Does everything have an answer?

Abnormality

What is abnormality?
Is it someone unlike yourself?
A person who is different?
Someone you think
Weird or strange
A target for your hate.

Is abnormality not being human
Or is it something unnatural?
Is it what the dictionary says
Or is it what you think it is?

Is there such thing as abnormality?
Is there such thing as normal?
Are you normal?
Am I abnormal?

To be different
Is normal
Neither you, nor I,
Nor anyone else Is
abnormal.

We are all different
In different ways
Not one of us
Is exactly the same
That is what makes us unique
Being unique is the norm.

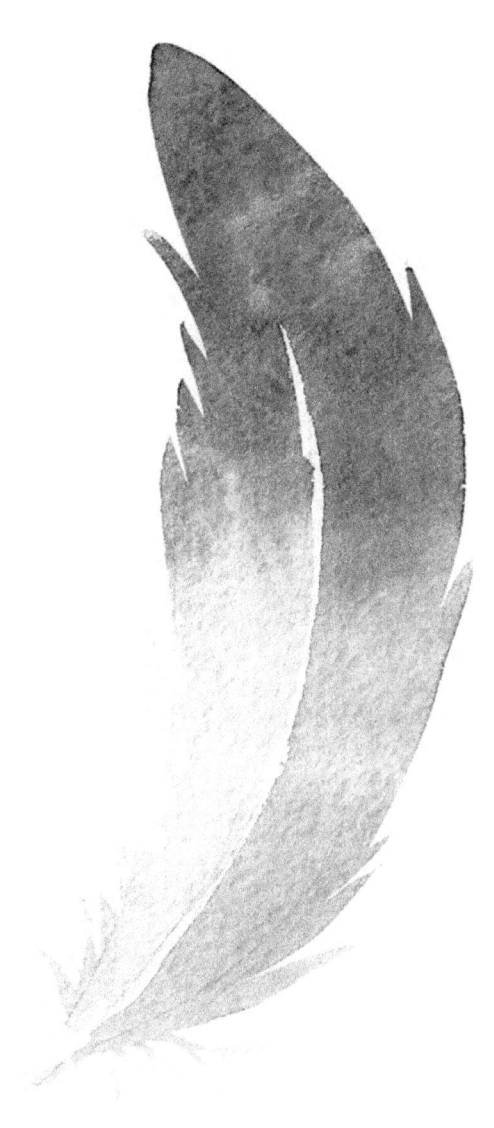

Matters of
The Heart

*When you engage your head and your heart,
Amazing things can happen.*

Love is Like a Disease

Love is like a disease
For which there is no cure
It is contagious
An addiction
No matter how hard you try
You can never quite
rid yourself of it
Love is like life
How it begins
and how it ends
You may never really understand
But you will fail to question it
Due to its amazing fulfilment.

Empty-Hearted

Where do the empty-hearted go,
What do they do
When all their love
All their hope is lost?

How do the empty-hearted feel
When their dearest family
Their closest friends,
Reject them?

Why are the empty-hearted left
Alone and deserted
When everyone else
Has love, hope, friendship and family
Close by all the time?

If you were the empty-hearted
Where would you go?
What would you do?
And how would you feel?
It would probably be
Just as negative as those
Neglected day after day.

Lonely Heart

I have a lonely heart
With no love left inside,
It has been ripped apart
No one cares.

This lonely heart Is lost
deep inside It does not
know
Where it is heading
It only knows
Where it has been.

My lonely heart
Has given up hope,
Is waiting to surrender
But still looking
For a way out.

This lonely heart
Is hiding away inside
Although used to rejection
Is afraid to face another
day.

Agonising Pain

Oh, the pain
Take this pain away
From this sensitive heart
It hurts so much
Does so much damage
To the heart and to the brain
This pain This agonising pain
Never healed.
Cries never noticed
Screams never heard
What is the use of expressing
What just isn't seen?
It is done
If words nor pictures
Can express what is felt
All that is left
Is pain.

Heartache

Heartache and pain take over your emotions
You cannot sleep
Tears often fall from your eyes
You get sudden feelings of loneliness,
Emptiness, regret and confusion
You try to make it go away
But it hurts even more
You try to understand
But you drive yourself insane
You start to lose control
Your self-esteem lowers
You feel endless pain
All throughout your body
You feel weak inside then out
Wish you could change things
But you feel hopeless
There is nothing you can do
You lose just one thing
But feel like you have lost everything
You do not want to go out and have fun
Instead you want to drown
In your own sorrow and tears.

See You Later

No one said
That life would be easy
One of the hardest things
Is losing someone you love
Heartache comes with sorrow
But you do not have to grieve alone
For though these times are hard
Know that there is a friend who cares
There is someone there to comfort you
Feel free to cry, to release your pain
Know in your heart that they loved you too
They are gone from us here
But there is a chance to meet again
This is only goodbye for now
And see you later.

Needs

Do not get tangled
With the hope of a friend,
It may all end up in pain.
Try to do the best for all
But keep yourself in mind.
Try not to neglect yourself
Just to please everyone else.
You have to do what is right
For everyone in sight.
You cannot leave one poor soul out,
For that is being unrealistic
To everyone involved.
Everyone needs to say
What they think must be done.
Do not try to take over
Or you'll be left alone.
So, when your friend needs a hand
Remember what needs to be done.

Inspiration

Many are inspired
By the hearts of others,
By the clever minds,
The ambitious souls.
Others are inspired
By the abilities of some,
By their strength and courage
Which are shown.
When one is inspired,
One learns to grow
Those who grow,
Become strong inside and out.
For inspiration strengthens the heart,
The mind, the body and the soul.

Always

Where would I be
If I didn't have you
To love me, treat me as a person?
I've always known
That you are the one
To care for and look after me
You were always there
From the start of my life
You've always been the one
To lift me up when I'm down
But I've never known
Just how to thank you
Yet, I've given you Love
and care in return
And I will never stop giving
As we grow even stronger together.
I will always remember
That you were the one
To really understand my life
For you are my one
And my only mother.

Saviour

It is in your presence
Where I fall to my knees
Lifting my voice to you
Nothing can tear me away from your love
You are everything I have
All I will ever need
Your son sent to die for all
In your name freely worship
My God, my everything
Praise to you alone
You provide hope, comfort
You rescued my soul
Lifted me out of despair
Soaring together side by side
You never leave
Always love
All I am is because of you
All I will ever be will be as you please
Life surrendered
Soul enflamed
Saviour, Lord
I am yours and you are mine.

A Friend For Life

When some ties are weakened and others break,
There are those that will be strengthened.

True Friendship

Friendship begins with a smile
The shake of a hand
Exchange of a glance.
Continue with sharing
A helping hand
One who is caring.
Friendship begins to grow
Two people draw nearer
Their love is support at all costs.
Friendship, the beginning
Of unconditional love
A journey far set
That will be accomplished.
Friendship withstands all battles,
Strong through storms and blizzards,
Grows with every disagreement
Bonds with the heartfelt touch of memory.
True friendship lives within us for eternity
Touching our hearts, minds and souls as one
Nothing extinguishes the power
Of true friendship.

Both Ways

I believe that friendship
Goes both ways.
As I believe that love
Goes both ways.
That trust with loyalty
Goes both ways.

If friendship, love and all within
Does not go both ways
Then, I believe
That it will not go in
The correct or wanted way.

Call on Me

Sometimes there are shady days
Cloudy overhead
Just remember
That it happens to us all
So when your sky is cloudy,
Call on me
I will be there.

You and Me

You help me through
My darkest days
And through my brightest days.
Without you,
I would be totally lost.
I need you here
Every day of my life
I love you so
As a very dear friend
Please reassure me
We will last forever
Because you and me
Friends for life
When everything else fails
Our friendship will survive.

Together Forever

You and I
Together forever
This friendship
We share
Special and rare
Just for
You and me.

Another Sister

What a friend I've found in you
A friend every girl prays for
Everyone desires
So lucky to have that friend
I can depend on
Despite time and distance
Like another sister
Not by blood, but by choice
A friendship formed many years ago
Growing day by day
Friends awhile
Friends forevermore.

Dearest Friend

How can I ever thank you
For all the ways you have helped me
You lifted me up
You boosted my spirits
You helped me keep
A smile on my face
Helped me stay focussed
On the truth.

The friend
I cherish the most
The friend
Most adored
You are a friend
That everyone deserves.

Eternity

Whenever you are down
And need a little hand
Always remember
That there is somewhere there
You have a friend in me
From now 'til eternity.

You and I will be
Together forever
So please have a heart
To stay here by my side
As I love you
Knowing you love me too.

Friends

Friends, those with
Unconditional love
Friends are there when
You need someone to talk to
Friends are there when
You need someone to hug
Friends are there with
Shoulders to cry on
Friends are there with
Hearts to trust and rely on
Friends are there
Through happy and sad
True friends remain
Within our hearts, it's stronger.

If I were an Angel

If I were an angel
I would watch over you
I would lie down beside you
Hush you to sleep
Calm all your fears.

If I were an angel
I would come down to comfort you
When times are troublesome
Watch you from above
When all things are well.

If I were an angel
I would promise you this
I would personally consult God
About your health and well-being
I would ask to be His messenger to you
I would visit you constantly
Always from above.

However, I am not an angel
But I am your friend
I promise to stay by your side
Whether you are weak or strong
Because God has called me
To be your friend, not your angel
As He made me human
Just like you.

Love:
A Partner
For Life

*"Therefore what God has joined together,
let no one separate."*

MARK 10:9 (NIV).

Memory of the Rose

Whoever thought that love
Could blossom from a simple rose
That is all it took for you
To steal my heart away.
From the first day I met you
Love swallowed up my heart
All that is left within me
Is the memory of the rose.

That rose with no thorns to hurt me
Your love touched my heart
Gentle and so passionate
The beautiful scent from the rose
Each moment of love fulfils my life
The part of me that was lost
Found again by a love
Which grew from a simple rose.

So sweet, so soft
Beautiful, so sensitive
Gentle tears of love
Liquid memory of that rose.

A rose may not last forever
But the love it gave me eternity fulfils
No other emotion so strong
No other emotion could capture
The heart and the soul as one
Nothing can extinguish this fire in my heart
For everything I feel leads me back
To the sweet memory of that rose.

Infatuation

I saw you there and knew it was you
We hadn't really met before
That first day we spoke
My heart started beating again
My face an instant glow
Joy in my life

Happiness became the bigger part of me
Now we're no more than friends
But the way you make me feel
So special and unique.
You held me close that first time
Every trouble floated away
Everything so perfect, I felt ok

When you let go of me
I felt a desire to hold you again
That feeling I had, I didn't want to end
The kiss on my cheek was so tender
I dreamt of that kiss on my lips
How I want you to be mine
But I don't know if you feel the same.

I want to be with you forever.
Is this love or just infatuation?
All I can think of is you
Don't leave me hanging here
Tell me how you feel
Do you feel the same way that I do
Or is this all in my head?

I have chosen to love you
I hope you choose to love me too.

Heart's Desire

When I met him, I was happy
While he was there, everything seemed ok
When he held me, I didn't want to let go
When he kissed my cheek,
I wished it was my lips
As soon as I saw him, I knew he was the one
He looked so gorgeous, adorable to me
He enlightened me in the instant
The rest of my day was a breeze
My thoughts, they always led back to him
When he left, I wanted to go with him
When I am with him, I feel so alive
Like nothing else matters, all is fulfilled
I think I am in love with him
Yet I fear it could just be infatuation
Does he really feel the same?
There is no one else I want
I desire him to be a part of my life
If love is a choice,
I choose to love
him and him alone.

Made Whole

It is all going to be ok
This I know
With a love so strong
Two lives combined
With complete understanding
A hope above all else
Where nothing stands in the way
Dreams and achievements are whole.

Two Hearts

No more, no less
Than loves first kiss
So soft and gentle
But never lost
So sweet and pure
Our hearts meet
One and another
Our hearts combine.

Be with Me

Together we could be forever
If you choose to be with me
We can make this love unique
And follow it through 'til the end
Love is everlasting
That's how our love should be
I am unwilling to ever let you go
For you've touched my life like no other
We are no longer two but one
And like this we can be forever
If you choose to be with me.

The Best Thing

When we made love
When I gave myself to you
A little pain was bearable
For a love so strongly ignited.
Whenever you touch me
I'm filled with the greatest sensations,
Only you can make me feel this way.
My life has just begun,
Before you, there was nothing
Now I have the best thing,
The best thing, that's you.
I'll go on smiling,
I'll keep my chin up,
I'll do it all for you.
I'll let the positives overtake the negatives,
You have taught me well,
Helped me learn what life is all about.
I have you to thank, I give you the credit
For turning my world around
For letting me be myself
And for helping me discover
The person I am inside.
When you hold me, all my troubles fade away
I have no cares in the world, nothing but you
Because the best thing that I have,
The best thing I have ever had,
The best thing for me
Is you!

Love

Love that is true
Lasting for eternity
Love for me
For everyone.

Love that is real
Through spirit, everlasting
Love, sacrifice
Laying down one's life for all.

Encountering The Spirit

*But from there you will seek the Lord your God,
and you will find Him if you seek Him
with all your heart and with all your soul.*

DEUTERONOMY 4:29 (NKJV).

Within Reach

I have a vision
A figure that is you
Standing in front of me
Not as a physical being
But your presence is tangible
By faith I reach out my hand
I can touch you.

I see the hand of God
Reaching down from Heaven
To touch each and every one.
He lays His hand on us
For comfort and healing
Healing that comes from the inside to the out
Absolute and pure.

You appear to me in my room
Clothed beautifully in white and gold
You stand with arms wide open
Beckoning me to come.

You call my name from a distance
But I hear it loud and clear
A photographic image in my mind
Sees you draw me close
And embrace me in a hug
In your loving arms I am truly home.

You are near, within reach
Though you are high above all else
Greater than any other
You come to be with us
And draw us near to you.

Tears for You

You bring a tear to my eye
Captured in your presence
In worship and in praise.
Tears in my eyes
I remember your good deeds
To bring you thanks.
Cry tears of joy
Instead of tears of pain.
Instead of tears out of fear
Shed tears of passion.
Shed tears of freedom
Granted by you through your son.
I am no longer ashamed of my tears
For they are an expression
Of my love for you
And my desire to know you more.

Intimate Spirit

Jesus set the mood
Something good is going to happen
A fire burning so strong
That cannot be contained
Captured by His presence
Caught up in His grace
An experience like no other
His Spirit falls in this place.

In the Moment

Through praise, through thanks, through prayer
An indescribable feeling
Overwhelmed by your presence
A burning sensation in my heart
Completely in the moment
Everything else is cast aside
All that remains is you.

I have the freedom
I lift up my hands
I give you praise
Fall to my knees
Total surrender to you
More alive than ever
My longing, only for you
Nothing else matters
In the moment with you.

Hidden

On the mountain top
In my darkest moment
You never left my side
You are the one I can trust
On you I can depend

You are so faithful
Very good to me
You saved my life, literally
Lead me from the wilderness
To our secret meeting places

You lay me down in your arms
Drenched in your peace
I am reminded why I love you
Because you love me, so tenderly
To me, are full of care

Now overwhelmed with joy
New fire burns within me
Longing for your presence
So long since I could say
I am happy, now I truly am

You quieten my soul
Now there is no need to escape
No will to run and hide
For I am hidden, in your arms
Safe and secure, I am okay

Finally, I feel like I can be me
Just as I am
No pressure, no expectation
Only grace
Only you.

Walk By Faith

*Our walk is different,
But our God is the same.*

Live and Let Live

Refuse to live for yourself
Instead live for God
He created and saved you
Put aside selfish desires
Set goals on something greater
Heart's desire for God
Do not dwell on earthly treasures
For none shall equal
What you will receive in Heaven
Have a warm, pure heart
Open your arms
Pray with thanks and pray for others
Before you consider yourself
Give as you've never given before
You will receive much greater things
Love God, love others and love yourself
And always remember to live and let live.

Follow God

Put full trust in the Lord
He will save you
Place all your fears
In the hands of the Lord
Give your life over
To your Heavenly Father
Stop living for yourself
And start living for God
When troubles arise
Turn directly to God
No one can help you
More than our Heavenly Father.
When your friend is not saved
Bring them to Jesus
When you have sinned
Confess to Jesus and repent
Whatever happens in your life
Whatever situations may occur
Turn to God in good and bad
Rely on someone you can trust
Have faith in someone you can love
Follow God
And may God lead the way.

Do Not Sin

Through your anger do not sin
Through disappointment and despair,
Through pain and suffering do not sin.

Hardships come upon us all
We cry, we hurt
But through these times, do not sin.

God looks upon us
God loves us unconditionally
Show your love for God in return.

May His will be done
Through Heaven and Earth
May all go according to His plan.

Your life is a special gift from God
May you dedicate it to Him forever
And seek to follow His ways.

Give your life to Jesus
Set forth to live for Him
For He will reign for all eternity.

Therefore, you shall not sin
If you suffer a fall from grace
Forgiveness lies in the heart of the Lord.

Falling Apart

Once again, my world is falling apart
But one thing is different this time
My faith in Jesus Christ
Whilst I may lose all that I have
I will not lose my faith
I will not give it up.
In the midst of everything
I have gained my faith
In the end of everything
My life will cease
What happened in the beginning?
How did it all begin?
I could say I was born
In the beginning of it all
But is that where it actually began?

When a life begins
There is no harsh emotional or mental pain
The hardest things a baby experiences
Are hunger, falls and separation
from its mother
But as life goes on the pain grows
It evolves and grows more intense
The most important thing is to focus on Jesus
Anything and everything is possible with faith
The world is falling apart
We cannot deal with ourselves
let alone the world
When many things fall apart at once
We do not know how to cope
We fall apart and we suffer even more
But we accept it as the way life goes
Jesus Christ has conquered all
Faith in him will lead us to harmony
Faith in him will change our lives.

I Choose

I choose to follow the Lord
To walk in His holiness
To fulfil His ways
In the path of Christianity
Choose to live for my God
Never to be beaten by evil
Stand firm for the Lord
To give my life to Jesus
Let love be my greatest aim
Pray without ceasing
Worship with all my heart
Choose to be who God chose me to be
To be no-one but whom God wants me to be
By the will of my God,
I choose one thing above all
To be me.

In The Wilderness

Faith alone is not enough
I cannot keep my head
above the waters
Lord, where are you now
In my time of need?

I am trying unsuccessfully to reach you
All you do is make me cry
And I need you so much right now
Please show me you are still here.

I cannot see you in me
I long to feel your
presence fill me up Lord,
won't you come to meet me
Let me encounter you again.

How do I know you are always here,
Yet have trouble believing it is true?
Why do I feel that you have left me,
Though your promise says you never will?

How can I think that life is not for me,
When you granted me eternal life through your son?
Why do I feel locked up in a prison, bound by chains
When you, yourself have set me free?

How long must I walk in the wilderness?
What will it take to regain my peace and my joy?
When will I receive my break-through
And start living again?

Lord, I need you
If you are not here, I am not living
You are my hope, my future
I refuse to walk without you.

Even though I do not feel you
Still you hold me close
You see me even now
As your heart breaks with mine.

In a time when trust seems difficult
Still I depend on you
Take my hand as I reach out to you
Remind me of your faithfulness.

In the valley of darkness, I wait for you
As I learn to fight with you, not against you
In time, my victory will come
And I will prosper, leaving this wilderness behind.

We Will Rise

As the eagle sits
With wings open wide
Looking straight ahead
Attention caught
By something in the distance
Focus not broken by anything
Sees what is coming
Prepares to rise
By the spirit of the Lord
Is lifted up and carried
To reach a higher level
Soar among the clouds
Nearer to Heaven.
As the eagle rises, we too will rise
Our focus upon the Lord
We will not be shaken
Will see His glory
On earth as in Heaven.
Soaring on the wind
Provided by His Spirit
We will reach new heights,
New levels and new perspectives
Here we will be enlightened
Seeing things
We do not yet see
We will see things
Those others do not see
The bigger picture will be revealed
Each of us significant in God's plan.

Through The Day

Through the hustle and bustle of my day
When nothing seems to go my way
When my thoughts and feelings are a mess
To you alone I must confess
As my troubles weigh me down
It is difficult to see your crown
Still, I seek you out in my distress
Lord show me today who I can bless
When life, to me, does not seem fair
Lord, may I come to you in prayer
Your word is the weapon that slays the demon
By your sacrifice I receive your freedom
And now I strive to fight for the cause
Of a Kingdom that is not mine, but yours.

Alphabetical Index

A Hopeless Pattern	34
A New Perspective	103
Abnormality	110
Afraid	57
Agonising Pain	117
All I Need	60
Always	122
Another Love	50
Another Sister	129
Anymore	33
Bad Influence	42
Be with Me	142
Both Ways	127
Call on Me	127
Choices	67
Christianity	3
Complete in You	39
Courage	77
Crossed the Line	47
Dearest Friend	130
Death	30
Desiderate	43
Do Not Sin	158
Do We Care?	107
Dreams	75
Dying Inside	31
Empty-Hearted	115
Eternity	131
Façade	71
Faith	105

Falling Apart	159
Fear	56
Feel	64
Follow God	157
Forgiveness	75
Friends	132
God is with Me	85
Hardships	76
Heart's Desire	140
Heartache	118
Heaven	30
Hidden	152
Hidden Talents	76
Him	45
His Way	46
Home Sweet Home	83
Hope	79
Hungry for You	21
I Believe	4
I Choose	161
I Forgive You	52
I Have Learnt	10
Identity	69
If I were an Angel	133
Imprisoned	27
In the Moment	151
In The Wilderness	162
Independent	65
Infatuation	138
Inspiration	121
Intimate Spirit	150
Is Seeing Believing?	109

Jesus Christ	6
Journey	12
Learning to Trust	87
Life	17
Life is Precious	19
Live and Let Live	156
Lonely Heart	116
Love	144
Love is Like a Disease	114
Made Whole	141
Memory of the Rose	136
Needs	120
Never Again	32
Never Let Me Go	91
No Words	97
Only You	82
Praise God	89
Ready	7
Relief	38
Rescued	93
Saviour	123
See You Later	119
Set Free	86
Solution?	15
Sometimes	100
Storm	28
Stuck	61
Success	74
Tears	79
Tears for You	150
The Best Thing	143
The End	35

They Don't Know	36
This Life	14
This World	101
Through The Day	165
Together Forever	128
Trapped	27
True Friendship	126
Two Hearts	141
Unwanted	5
Voices	62
Want To Know	26
We Will Rise	164
What Changed	49
What?	29
Whenever I Need Someone	84
Who?	83
Wish	37
Within Reach	148
Woman	66
You	51
You and Me	128
Young Lives for You	95

www.ingramcontent.com/pod-product-compliance
Lightning Source LLC
Chambersburg PA
CBHW071449080526
44587CB00014B/2049